Worry Therapy

Worry Therapy

written by
Daniel Grippo

illustrated by
R.W. Alley

ONE
CARING
PLACE

Abbey Press

Text © 2000 by Daniel Grippo
Illustrations © 2000 by St. Meinrad Archabbey
Published by One Caring Place
Abbey Press
St. Meinrad, Indiana 47577

Library of Congress Catalog Number
00-103683

ISBN 978-0-87029-345-0

Printed in the United States of America

Foreword

Do you worry too much? Are you often anxious or apprehensive? Not to worry. This little book can provide just the relief you need.

We all worry—about our families, work, finances, health, the challenges of everyday life. But prolonged or extreme worry is destructive. Not only does it feel uncomfortable, but it can also make us more prone to physical ailments and rob us of the joy of living. Plus, the mental energy wasted on worrying can weaken our ability to take needed action.

Whether you feel chronically bogged down in worry or are facing an immediate crisis, *Worry Therapy* can help. This little guide offers practical hints for "worry-proofing" your life, as well as insights into deeper issues. With clever illustrations and uplifting thoughts, it will guide you toward the attitude adjustment and spiritual surrender that can considerably ease your burdens.

So relax...read...and let this little book lead the way from worry to restored serenity!

1.

Worry is like the rain—a little can be good; too much is destructive. Like a gentle rain, worry can be a gift from God, letting us know life is out of balance and needs fixing.

2.

Sometimes worry isn't so gentle. It pours down so hard we feel as if we're drowning in it. Yet we can learn to channel worry in positive directions.

3.

Just as we can weatherproof a house, we can take steps to "worry-proof" our lives. We can't stop the worry from coming (or the rain from falling), but we <u>can</u> make sure we have shelter when it hits.

4.

Make a list of what worries
you. When you get worries off
your chest and onto paper, you
take away some of their power.
You can begin to look at them
more objectively.

5.

Look at your Worry List and ask, "What's my biggest worry today?" Circle it. Ask yourself, "What can I do to lessen this concern today?" Then do it.

6.

Be sure to focus on what you can do, not on what you <u>can't</u>. It will help you to realize that you do have choices and to come up with creative solutions.

Home Health
Care Services

7.

Too often we only think about what's wrong in our lives. Next time you face a worrisome situation, ask yourself, "What's right here?" Balance your worries with hope and optimism.

8.

Make another list. Call it your
"Just Fine List." As you ponder
all the things that are okay
with your life, you may find
that your Just Fine List dwarfs
your Worry List.

JUST FINE LIST
1. Garden doesn't need water.
2. Birdbath is full.
3. Drainpipes are clean.

9.

Get going on a worrisome task early in the day. That way, it loses its power to hold the rest of your day captive.

10.

It's easy to imagine the worst, but the worst rarely happens. Most of the time things work out just fine—whether we've worried about them or not. Try not to "awfulize."

11.

When you're feeling overwhelmed by the "what ifs" ("What if _x_ goes wrong?" "What if _y_ happens?"), it's time for some backup planning. Assume the thing you're worried about <u>does</u> in fact happen. What will you do? What will you need?

12.

When we crowd our schedules
with too many commitments,
we create opportunities for
increased tension. Try slowing
down your day. Space out your
commitments...leave gaps in
your schedule...give yourself
a little breathing room.

13.

Being a worrywart involves constantly visualizing bad things happening. Redirect your imagination and visualize positive outcomes. Once you can visualize something good happening, you can look forward to it.

14.

If you're worried about something big in the future, plan ahead. What small steps can you take now to help you cut a big worry down to size?

15.

Worries multiply when we're scattered and unfocused. Try to do one thing at a time. When you concentrate on the task at hand—no matter how great or small—you leave less room for worry to take hold.

16.

Worry thrives on the feeling of helplessness. Don't hesitate to ask for the help you need. Your burdens will be lightened.

17.

Many worriers have trouble delegating. When we realize others are able to carry some of our responsibilities, we can share the load. And the whole world isn't on our shoulders anymore. What a relief!

18.

Listen to your "self-talk"—the messages you send yourself. Are you telling yourself, "I'll never succeed at anything," or "I'm always messing things up"? Eliminate negative self-talk and watch worry wither away.

19.

Some of the things we worry about are beyond our own ability to fix. When you're feeling overwhelmed by a problem, invite God into the situation through prayer.

20.

Try using distraction in situations that make you uncomfortable. Some people who worry about flying, for example, take an engrossing novel with them. Engage your mind in something more intriguing than worry.

21.

There are few worries that can outlast a luxurious bubble bath, a dip in a whirlpool, or a hot shower. Let warm water bring soothing comfort while you take a break from your worries. As you allow your body to relax, notice how your worries lose their grip on you.

22.

"Don't sweat the small stuff"
is great advice for worrywarts.
But working up a sweat is still
a good idea, because exercise
allows your body to release all
sorts of stored-up stress. Get a
move on—outrun your worries!

23.

Gentle music can soothe a troubled soul. When was the last time you took in a string quartet, a classical guitar concert, or gentle piano music? Find peaceful music that suits your tastes, and keep it near at hand whenever worry starts to disturb the peace.

24.

Laughter is the best medicine for many ailments, including excessive worry. Take in a funny movie or play; call a friend who makes you laugh; read the cartoons in the paper. Laughter can brighten a day clouded with worry. Let the sun shine!

25.

"Sleep…knits up the ravell'd sleave of care" and is the "balm of hurt minds," said Shakespeare. Getting enough rest at night is essential when you're feeling overcome by worry. And don't overlook the healing power of a catnap. After all, when was the last time you saw a cat that looked worried?

26.

Eat well and wisely—don't add poor nutrition or overeating to your worries. Make meals a time to socialize, to enjoy the company of family and friends, to celebrate life.

27.

Spend time in the great outdoors and observe nature at work. The grandeur of creation has a way of shrinking worries. Take a walk and tell worry to take a hike!

28.

Whether you're playing the piano, woodworking, fixing a car, or painting a sunset—when you engage in a hobby, life becomes engaging. The more engaging life is, the less worrisome it is.

29.

Seek out optimistic people. Naysayers bring nothing but worry. Positive and hopeful people bring balm to a troubled soul.

30.

Divide your worries in half by sharing them with a trusted confidant. Just getting them out into the open often lessens the load. Plus, you may gain a fresh, more objective perspective on the situation, leading to new solutions.

31.

When you get in touch with
a good friend, you get in touch
with the goodness, beauty, and
strength inside yourself.
Cultivate the garden of
friendship and there will be
less room for the weeds of
worry to take root.

32.

If you dwell in the past, you invite regrets. If you dwell in the future, you invite worry. When you dwell in the present, you invite delight, because the present moment is filled with nothing but wonder!

33.

Help a neighbor with the groceries. Volunteer to teach a child to read. Visit an ailing friend in the hospital. When you get outside yourself, worry doesn't know where to find you.

34.

Some of us, by temperament, are more prone to worry. And we need extra effort to keep it in check. Know your own warning signs when worry is throwing you off balance, and take immediate steps to steady yourself.

35.

Worry thrives in a noisy environment. Take some quiet time for yourself. Turn down the volume and listen for the calm, still voice at your center. There…isn't that better?

36.

Given life's many uncertainties, a certain amount of worrying is unavoidable. But if you let God be in charge, you will find that you don't have to control life— you only have to live it. Let God be God.

37.

Remember, God wants only the best for you, and will either relieve you of your worry or give you the strength to bear it. Give your worries to God...again... and again...and again.

38.

Don't let worry get the best of you—get the best of worry. Use it as a springboard to take needed action, improve your outlook, and get your life in balance.

Daniel Grippo is an editor and publisher now living in Mexico. He has written on a variety of spiritual and religious topics over the years and can be reached at <u>writingdan@yahoo.com</u>.

Illustrator for the Abbey Press Elf-help Books, **R.W. Alley** also illustrates and writes children's books. He lives in Barrington, Rhode Island, with his wife, daughter, and son. See a wide variety of his works at: <u>www.rwalley.com</u>.

The Story of the Abbey Press Elves

The engaging figures that populate the Abbey Press "elf-help" line of publications and products first appeared in 1987 on the pages of a small self-help book called *Be-good-to-yourself Therapy*. Shaped by the publishing staff's vision and defined in R.W. Alley's inventive illustrations, they lived out author Cherry Hartman's gentle, self-nurturing advice with charm, poignancy, and humor.

Reader response was so enthusiastic that more Elf-help Books were soon under way, a still-growing series that has inspired a line of related gift products.

The especially endearing character featured in the early books—sporting a cap with a mood-changing candle in its peak—has since been joined by a spirited female elf with flowers in her hair.

These two exuberant, sensitive, resourceful, kindhearted, lovable sprites, along with their lively elfin community, reveal what's truly important as they offer messages of joy and wonder, playfulness and co-creation, wholeness and serenity, the miracle of life and the mystery of God's love.

With wisdom and whimsy, these little creatures with long noses demonstrate the elf-help way to a rich and fulfilling life.

Elf-help Books

...adding "a little character" and a lot
of help to self-help reading!